THE WRITING MANIFESTO

WRITING JOURNAL

Published By The Writing Manifesto®

www.thewritingmanifesto.org